CAPTURED
SCIENCE
HISTORY

MARS ROVER

HOW A SELF-PORTRAIT CAPTURED THE POWER OF *CURIOSITY*

by Danielle Smith-Llera

Content Adviser: Frank Summers, PhD
Outreach Astrophysicist
Space Telescope Science Institute

COMPASS POINT BOOKS
a capstone imprint

Compass Point Books are published by Capstone,
1710 Roe Crest Drive, North Mankato, Minnesota 56003
www.mycapstone.com

Editor: Catherine Neitge
Designers: Tracy Davies McCabe and Catherine Neitge
Media Researcher: Svetlana Zhurkin
Library Consultant: Kathleen Baxter
Production Specialist: Laura Manthe

Image Credits
NASA: 47, 56 (left), 57 (top), ESA/A. Dyer, 15, JPL, 18–19, 20–21, 22, 23, 25, 45, 56
(right), 57 (bottom), 59 (bottom), JPL/Cornell University, 58 (right), JPL/Malin Space
Science Systems, 9, JPL/Pioneer Aerospace, 37, JPL-Caltech, 6–7, 11, 27, 28, 31,
35, 39, 41, 43, 46, 49, 59 (top), JPL-Caltech/ASU/UA, 33, JPL-Caltech/Dan Goods,
17, JPL-Caltech/MSSS, cover, 13, 50, 53, 58 (left), JPL-Caltech/MSSS/TAMU, 55;
Newscom: Reuters/Andrew Burton, 5, Reuters/Fred Prouser, 34; Science Source, 16

Library of Congress Cataloging-in-Publication Data
Cataloging-in-publication information is on file with the Library of Congress.
ISBN 978-0-7565-5641-9 (library binding)
ISBN 978-0-7565-5645-7 (paperback)
ISBN 978-0-7565-5649-5 (ebook pdf)

Printed in the United States of America.
010374F17

TABLEOFCONTENTS

ChapterOne
SEVEN TERRIFYING MINUTES

Hundreds of people crowded into New York's Times Square, looking up at a huge screen after midnight on August 6, 2012. They were hoping to see the next chapter in space exploration unfold. Many more watched in science center auditoriums across the United States. Millions watched online, hoping for a glimpse of the surface of the planet that appears as a red dot in Earth's sky. Whether this chapter would end with triumph or disaster was anyone's guess.

Almost nine months earlier, the U.S. National Aeronautics and Space Administration (NASA) had launched a spacecraft toward Mars with a wheeled robot packed inside. For a decade, engineers working on the Mars Science Lab mission labored over the design and construction of the one-ton rover, which was named *Curiosity*. The rover rests low on six wide wheels. Scientific instruments are attached to its body, and some cluster at the end of a mechanical arm. Lenses and instruments mounted on its mast suggest a face. The size of a small car, the rover cost almost $2.5 billion, "the price of a movie ticket for every person in the United States," according to mission geochemist Roger Wiens. "The public would get its money's worth."

NASA invited the world to share the triumph—or

A crowd in New York City's Times Square celebrated as the rover *Curiosity* made its way to the surface of Mars in 2012.

catastrophe—of the mission as it was happening. TV cameras at NASA's Jet Propulsion Laboratory (JPL) in Pasadena, California, beamed live images from mission control. There, team members wearing blue polo shirts sat at several rows of monitors. Systems engineer Allen Chen was ready to narrate the coming events for both his team and audiences around the world. *Curiosity* was almost at the end of its 345-million-mile (555-million-kilometer) interplanetary voyage. But the greatest challenge was ahead: It had to survive a 7-minute plunge through the Martian atmosphere and land safely. "I worked 10 years for seven minutes to go well," Chen said.

Would *Curiosity* survive the drop and land on its wheels, ready to roam and explore? Or would it suffer the fate of previous Mars missions, which had shot past the planet, crashed, or simply stopped communicating? Since 1960, more than half of all missions to the red planet had failed. "We've got literally seven minutes to get from the top of the atmosphere to the surface of Mars, going from 13,000 miles an hour to zero in perfect sequence, perfect choreography, perfect timing," engineer Tim Rivellini said in a NASA video about the mission. "If any one thing doesn't work just right, it's game over." Mars Science Lab mission engineer Adam Steltzner worried that the entire mission rode on his Entry, Descent and Landing (EDL) team, the people responsible for depositing the rover safely on Mars. "It's kind of an emotional time," he said. "We're wishing for the best. We feel that we've done everything to deserve it, and now it's in the hands of the fates."

As *Curiosity*'s capsule neared Mars, the planet's gravity drew it in. *Curiosity* navigated downward blindly most of the way. Its cameras and radar were packed inside the capsule's darkness. A NASA orbiter tracked the capsule and sent updates about the descent as radio signals to Earth. Engineers

An artist's concept of NASA's Mars Science Laboratory's spacecraft approaching Mars with *Curiosity* safely tucked inside

could translate this "heartbeat" to learn the capsule's speed, altitude, and path toward the surface. Chen announced reassuringly, "Things are looking good."

Now more like spectators, mission members monitored the unfolding drama. A spacecraft takes months to travel from Earth to Mars, and it takes "14 minutes or so for the signal from the spacecraft to make it to Earth—that's how far Mars is away from us," Steltzner explained. *Curiosity*'s team could not guide the rover's high-speed descent from Earth with that much delay. So engineers had programmed *Curiosity* with 500,000 lines of computer code so it could operate on its own and steer itself to the rocky surface of the planet. Now the team only needed to send the simple command "Do_EDL"—and wait. Because of the delay, the spacecraft had already completed its descent when the JPL team got the signal saying the descent had started.

Chen's updates were beamed around the world. *Curiosity*'s capsule hit Mars' atmosphere, tearing along at 13,000 mph (20,920 kph). In just over a minute, friction spiked its temperature to 2,372 degrees Fahrenheit (1,300 degrees Celsius). But though it glowed brightly, relieved engineers learned that its heat shield had not burned away.

Chen announced that the capsule's parachute had deployed to slow the plummeting craft. Applause swept through the room around him. The parachute weighed only about 100 pounds (45 kilograms), but it could withstand 65,000 pounds (29,500 kg) of force. And there was more good news: The capsule's speed had fallen dramatically, to 200 mph (320 kph).

Having served its purpose, the heat shield needed to be discarded. Keeping it would have made a safe landing impossible. Mission engineer Steve Lee said

CURIOSITY'S EYES

Michael Malin is the subject of a test photo at JPL by a Mastcam of his design.

Spacecraft photographs have told Mars' story to Earthlings since 1965. The *Mariner* spacecraft were originally designed without cameras, but mission scientists thought they would be beneficial and they were added. Today onboard cameras are prized. Seventeen cameras are aboard *Curiosity*. NASA selected Michael Malin to design *Curiosity*'s main cameras. The former professor and JPL scientist has worked on spacecraft cameras since 1986. "His cameras had taken literally millions of pictures from spacecraft launched to the Red Planet," said geochemist Roger Wiens. "He seemed to know every square foot of Mars like his own backyard."

As soon as *Curiosity*'s heat shield fell away, one of Malin's cameras started clicking. The Mars Descent Imager snapped nearly 300 photographs, making the first movie of a Mars landing. The Mastcam designed by Malin is two cameras mounted 7 feet (2 m) above the surface on a rotatable mast. They take crisp, colorful photographs that can be woven into dramatic 360-degree views. Each camera "sees" differently; one can focus narrowly while the other sees a wider perspective. Mission engineer Adam Steltzner said that when images from both "eyes" are combined, "humans can relate to the distances just like as if they were there." With the help of the images, scientists can guide the rover toward interesting rocks to investigate.

Curiosity has a 7-foot (2-m) robotic arm that holds another Malin-designed camera called the Mars Hand Lens Imager (MAHLI). It does the same job as the magnifying lens that geologists on Earth wear around their necks. MAHLI can photograph objects smaller than a human hair. Close-up photographs showing the colors and structure of rocks can help scientists learn how they formed.

they had to "get that heat shield off. It's like a big lens cap blocking our view of the ground to the radar." Chen announced to applause, "We are in powered flight." Team members knew that meant the heat shield had dropped away and rockets had fired to fly *Curiosity* away from the parachute. Radar directed the craft toward its target near the base of Mount Sharp in Gale Crater.

The landing was going according to plan, yet an enormous challenge was just ahead. NASA had used parachutes and rockets on Mars landings before, but it had never used a sky crane maneuver. To land the massive rover, *Curiosity* would first hover just 65 feet (20 meters) above the ground. Cables would then lower the rover. When its wheels rested on Mars soil, explosives would fire and cut the cables, freeing the rover from the sky crane, which would soar off to crash far away. "If it went well," said Steltzner, "we'd be lauded as brainiac, brilliant guys, and if it went poorly we would be obvious idiots."

At 10:31 p.m. Pacific Daylight Time on August 5, 2012, Chen made the announcement that everyone had been waiting for: "Touchdown confirmed. We're safe on Mars." Team members leapt up cheering, hugged one another, laughed and cried. In an auditorium at JPL, members of the many teams who had worked on *Curiosity* celebrated along with audiences around the world. "*Curiosity* was designed

"If it went well, we'd be lauded as brainiac, brilliant guys, and if it went poorly we would be obvious idiots."

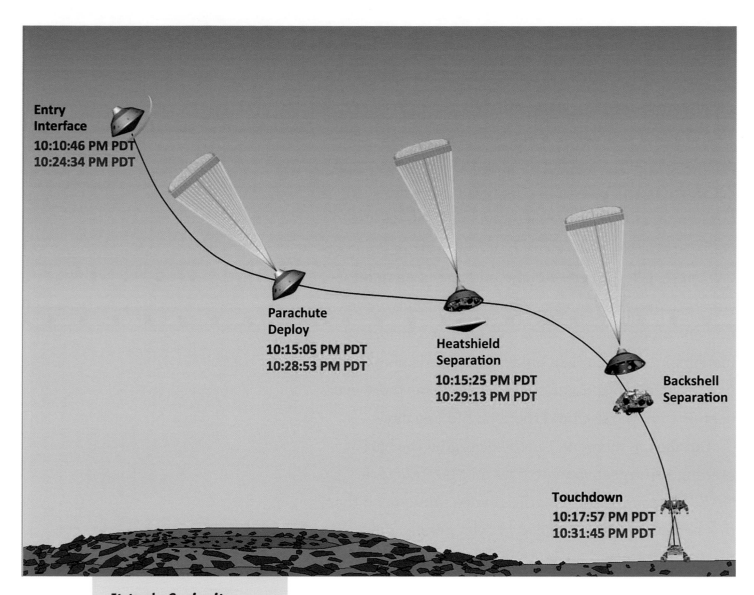

Entry
Interface
10:10:46 PM PDT
10:24:34 PM PDT

Parachute
Deploy
10:15:05 PM PDT
10:28:53 PM PDT

Heatshield
Separation
10:15:25 PM PDT
10:29:13 PM PDT

Backshell
Separation

Touchdown
10:17:57 PM PDT
10:31:45 PM PDT

It took *Curiosity* 7 minutes, 11 seconds to land on Mars from its entry point. The times the events occurred are in red. The times that Earth received confirmation are in blue.

and built to live on Mars and she is home now," said mission scientist R. Aileen Yingst.

A message from *Curiosity* soon arrived. It was an image. "All we could see at first was that the light part of the image was up and the dark part was down," recalled Wiens. "It was enough to confirm that *Curiosity* had landed right-side up." A second image followed. Rover wheels on Martian soil! For Steltzner, the images were ample reward for years of work—"a new image from a new place in our universe is what we do it for and what really fills us."

Curiosity's cameras would go on to take many photos, including self-portraits of the rover sitting on Martian soil, panoramic images of the Mars landscape, and a photo of a patch of gravel, in vivid color and detail. *Curiosity*'s first self-portrait came on day three, a 360-degree image taken by a navigation camera. Many full-length selfies would follow. The images, along with the data collected by *Curiosity*'s instruments, would help answer questions people have been curious about for centuries: Has there ever been life on Mars? Could there be life one day?

But for the moment, Earth celebrated the feat of landing its largest robot to date on Mars' surface. NASA Administrator Charlie Bolden announced that this achievement would lead to even greater ones. "Today, right now," he said, "the wheels of *Curiosity* have begun to blaze the trail for human footprints on Mars."

Curiosity's self-portraits on Mars have delighted rover fans with its humanlike features. "This is exactly what you or I would do if we were traveling, if we were going someplace new and exciting … we would take our phone" and shoot pictures, said Yingst. "This is essentially what the rover is doing for us here."

"Today, right now, the wheels of *Curiosity* have begun to blaze the trail for human footprints on Mars."

The self-portrait of *Curiosity* was a compilation of many images taken by the camera at the end of the rover's robotic arm.

ChapterTwo
FOLLOW THE WATER

Long before NASA sent spacecraft to study Mars, people used their eyes alone to peer up at the red dot in the night sky. The Egyptians named it Har Decher—the red one. Its bloody color led Babylonians to call it Nergal—the king of conflicts. The Romans named it Mars after their god of war.

By the 1500s, scientists wanted to understand more about Mars than its striking color. In 1576 Danish astronomer Tycho Brahe set up an observatory. For the next 20 years he used his keen eyesight and large instruments to study Mars' path through the night sky. In 1609, the Italian astronomer Galileo used a simple telescope to observe Mars but saw only a bright, featureless disc.

Better-designed telescopes brought Mars into sharper focus. Dutch astronomer Christiaan Huygens discovered a white spot at Mars' south pole in 1672. By 1719, astronomer Giacomo Miraldi wondered whether the white areas at the two poles were ice. (They are.) For the next three centuries, people debated whether there was water —and therefore life—on Mars.

Astronomers were eager to discover clues of life on Mars. Larger telescopes housed inside observatories cropped up around the world in the

Mars shines brightly in the night sky.

1800s. Astronomers drew maps of the light and dark areas they could see on the planet's surface. Some imagined the dark areas were oceans flowing around light-colored continents. Italian astronomer Giovanni Schiaparelli began mapping Mars in 1877. He saw

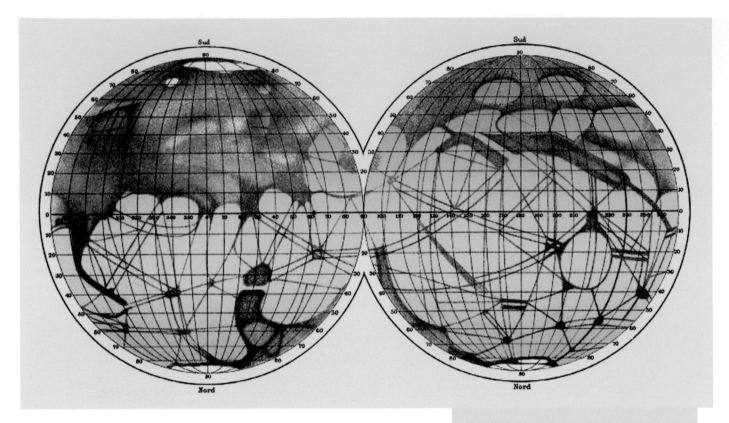

streaks on its surface that seemed like channels. Amateur astronomer Percival Lowell argued in 1895 that these marks were a network of water-filled canals, built by intelligent inhabitants.

Earthlings saw Mars up close for the first time in 1965. JPL helped launch *Mariner 4*, a probe designed to study Mars. Its two antennas and four solar panels sprouted from a frame holding several instruments, including a camera. On July 14, 1965, it swept past Mars, taking pictures. It took a week for the 22 black-and-white images to travel back to Earth as radio waves. Today *Curiosity* sends data at a rate almost 250,000 times as fast. *Mariner* team members were so eager to make sure its images arrived safely

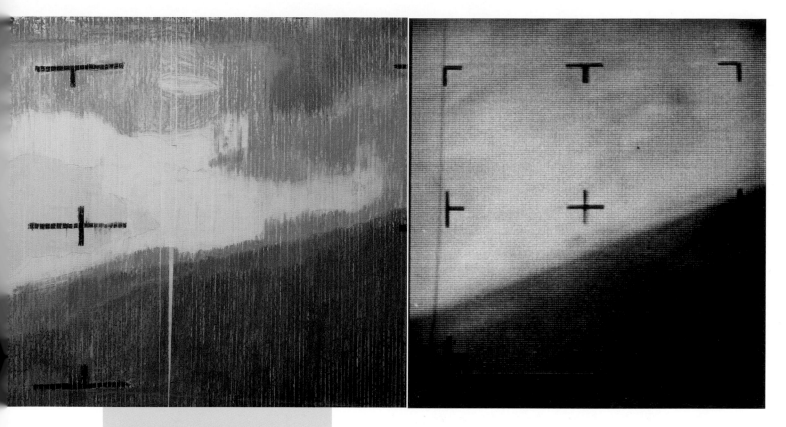

JPL engineers created a colored hand-drawn image of *Mariner 4*'s first actual photo from Mars.

that they instructed the probe to send them twice.

People had wondered for decades whether Mars was an inviting place. But *Mariner 4*'s eagerly awaited images only revealed a desert studded with rocks and, in some places, craters. The probe's instruments found that Mars' atmosphere was too thin to hold much warmth or to protect the planet from the sun's dangerous electromagnetic radiation. In short, Mars seemed hostile to life.

The urge to explore Mars was not crushed, but scientists would need more than a probe to study Mars. In its brief fly-by, *Mariner 4* had taken images of just 1 percent of Mars. NASA scientists needed to take better photographs to see whether Mars

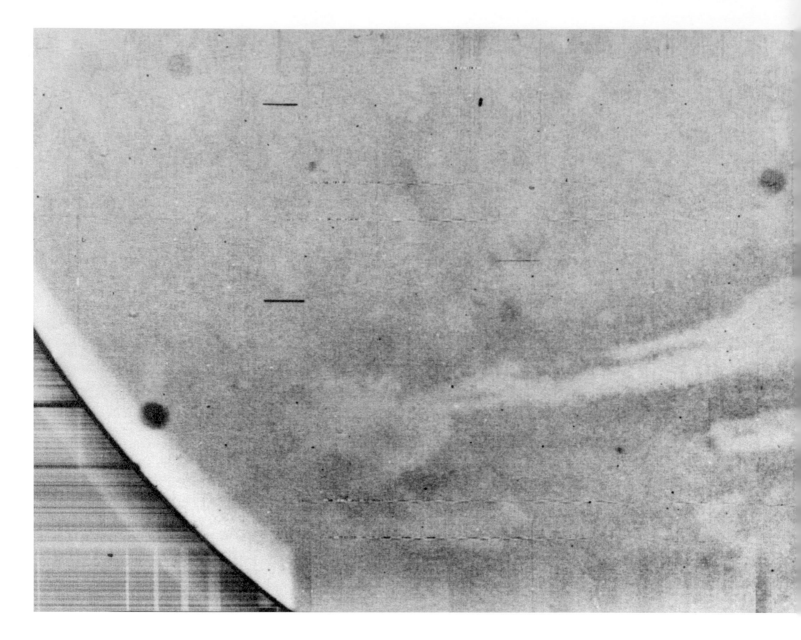

held water. On Earth, water is an essential part of chemical reactions that keep organisms alive—from humans to trees to bacteria. Without water, humans cannot digest food, move, or breathe. If water flows, or once flowed, on Mars, then some form of life could exist, or might have once existed.

NASA's next step was to send an orbiter,

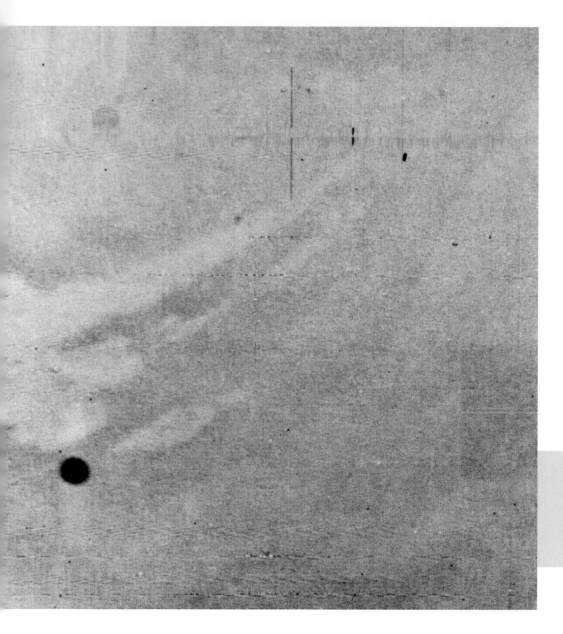

Mariner 9 photographed a canyon system emerging from a Martian dust storm.

Mariner 9. It began orbiting Mars on November 13, 1971, and studied the planet for nearly a year. It took thousands of photographs, which showed more than an empty landscape with swirling dust storms. Volcanoes towered high above the surface, and a massive canyon ran 3,000 miles (4,830 km) across the planet.

Yet the most exciting discovery was Mars' surface. Images showed a landscape possibly carved by ancient rivers. Geologists know that rocks reflect the history of a place. They can be shaped by the erosion of wind and water and transformed by heat and pressure. On Earth, geologists study rocks in their natural settings and take samples back to their labs. Astronauts collected more than 800 pounds (365 kg) of surface samples when they visited the moon in 1969, 1971, and 1972. But carrying out this work so far from Earth, in Mars' harsh environment, was impossible at that time. Instead, scientists would have to send a robot to Mars. Landers would be the next step in the planet's exploration.

The first of two *Viking* landers touched down on Mars on July 20, 1976, with the help of a heat shield, parachute, and rockets. Its first black-and-white image showed the lander's footpad resting on the rocky ground. A wide view of the landscape followed. The lander took the first color photograph from Mars the next day, and it was broadcast on television. *Viking 1* sent images and data back to Earth for six years, and its twin, *Viking 2*, sent them for almost four. Using data from the landers, scientists studied wind speeds, temperatures, and changes in moisture throughout Martian seasons. They discovered that iron-rich clay dust swirling in the atmosphere and coating the surface gave the planet its rusty color and the atmosphere its pink haze.

The *Viking 1* lander took the first photograph from the Martian surface on July 20, 1976.

The *Viking* landers' cameras were geologists' eyes and magnifying lenses. Scoops at the end of their robotic arms were like scientists' hands. The landers contained miniature, simplified versions of scientific labs on Earth. Each lander's lab could conduct three experiments on soil samples, looking for gases and chemicals indicating that microscopic living matter was present. But they found no liquid water and no clear evidence of microorganisms. They detected methane gas, which is produced by life forms. But the findings didn't show whether there was life on Mars.

Scientists believe a photo from *Viking 2* reflects the true colors of the Martian surface and sky.

But what if clues lay beyond the reach of the stationary lander's robotic arms? Scientists needed mobile robots called rovers to explore interesting locations beyond their landing sites. But robots were expensive. They required costly materials that would work in space and many skilled teams to design, build, and test them. After the popular human missions to the moon had ended, money for space exploration had grown scarce.

COMPETITION TO COOPERATION

When the Soviets launched *Sputnik*, Earth's first artificial satellite, into orbit in 1957, the Americans scrambled to catch up. It was the beginning of the Space Race. The U.S. government turned to the Jet Propulsion Laboratory. JPL was founded by a group of young California Institute of Technology scientists who had been experimenting with rockets since the 1930s. Less than three months after the Soviet launch, JPL built the first U.S. satellite. *Explorer 1* was launched in January 1958. Later that year NASA was founded, and JPL, which had been sponsored by the U.S. Army, was transferred to the newly formed agency. The mission of JPL, which is managed by Caltech, is the robotic exploration of space.

NASA has had great success with missions to Mars. But the Soviets were the first to land on the planet. The Soviets used a heat shield, parachute, and rockets to safely deposit a lander on Mars' surface on December 2, 1971. It was the first craft to survive on Mars long

In releasing an image in 1958, NASA said, "America joined the space race with the launch of this small, but important spacecraft."

enough to send a transmission, although the transmission lasted only 14.5 seconds.

Today American and Russian instruments work side by side on *Curiosity*. Russia's space agency contributed the neutron spectrometer. An instrument once used to make nuclear weapons, it now helps the rover detect water.

NASA embarked on a plan to explore space with less money in 1992. New spacecraft would carry just a few instruments. Scientists would compete to design the best cameras and tools in the least expensive way possible. Then NASA could send more daring missions to space and do it more often. One bold plan was to send a lander along with a rover to roll around Mars. It would cost much less than the *Viking* mission had cost two decades earlier.

The glowing heat shield of a space capsule burst through the Martian atmosphere on July 4, 1997. A parachute and rockets slowed the fall of the *Pathfinder* lander, which had a tiny rover, only 12 inches (30 centimeters) tall, tucked inside. Weighing just 23 pounds (10.5 kg), the wheeled robot was named after antislavery crusader Sojourner Truth. Explosives fired to inflate a cluster of airbags that surrounded *Sojourner* like a bunch of grapes. About 40 feet (12 m) from the surface, the device dropped to the ground and bounced powerfully until it rolled to a stop. The bags deflated, and protective panels opened like petals. The six-wheeled rover soon rolled down its ramp, powered by the solar panel on its back. The toylike robot charmed fans around the world who followed its adventures online.

Sojourner never went farther than 40 feet (12 m) from its lander, and it traveled only 330 feet (100 m) during its months-long mission. But among the

The *Pathfinder* lander photographed *Sojourner* on the rocky surface of the Mars landing site. Scientists believe the rocks and pebbles were washed down in an ancient flood.

thousands of photographs taken by the lander and rover, scientists found strong evidence that water had once flowed on the planet. The evidence included rocks with rounded edges, possibly caused by ancient floods. The evidence suggested that Mars was once a warmer, wetter world.

Two embarrassing failures shook NASA's confidence in 1999. First an orbiter was lost during an attempt to enter Mars' orbit in September. About two months later, a lander designed to dig for ice near the planet's south pole was lost during descent. NASA was more cautious with future missions. Scientists would send twin rovers to Mars, which would double their chances of a safe landing and of finding evidence of water. In January 2004, parachutes, rockets, and airbags deposited two identical landers the size of golf carts on Mars. *Spirit* and *Opportunity* landed on opposite sides of the planet, three weeks apart. Cameras topping masts 5 feet (1.5 m) tall could take photographs—from a human height—of the rovers' solar-paneled backs. Other cameras captured Mars' miles-high dust devils.

But where was the water? For years, the rovers searched plains, hills, basins, and craters. *Spirit* traveled almost 5 miles (8 km) before getting stuck in sand in May 2009. *Opportunity* has logged the greatest distance traveled on another planet, reaching 27.2 miles (43.8 km) in early 2017. And it is still traveling. Mission team members have received hundreds of thousands of images documenting the journey. They range from sweeping views from hilltops to data charts showing the minerals making up a rock.

For geologists, the images help fill in a portrait of ancient Mars. For example, *Spirit* took an image of its

Mars rovers got bigger through the years. A twin of *Sojourner* is in front. Test rovers for *Spirit* and *Opportunity* (left) and *Curiosity* flanked two engineers at JPL's Mars Yard testing area in Pasadena, California.

wheel tracks, which uncovered white material under the red dust. Scientists were surprised to identify silica, a compound that forms in high heat. While Mars today has an average temperature of -81 F (-63 C), silica suggests that Mars may once have bubbled with hot springs.

The rovers' photos tell geologists that a great deal of water was once on Mars. *Opportunity*'s photos of layered rocks suggest that flowing water dropped

"We think *Opportunity* is parked on what was once the shoreline of a salty sea on Mars."

sand that slowly hardened into rock. Over time, more layers were deposited and hardened. These sedimentary rocks hold a record of Mars' ancient rivers, lakes, and floods. Photos of small spheres of hematite embedded in rock also intrigued geologists. The reddish mineral forms in ground soaked in salt water. "We think *Opportunity* is parked on what was once the shoreline of a salty sea on Mars," said mission scientist Steve Squyres.

"There was a lot of water beneath the ground," he said. "You wouldn't want to drink this stuff. But there was this acidic water beneath the ground." Did this evidence of water on Mars mean there had been life too? Maybe. It was "not exactly an evolutionary paradise," said Squyres. "There was acid. It was dry much of the time, but it's the kind of environment that would have been definitely suitable for some simple forms of life."

Images streaming back from robots and orbiters continue to inspire scientists interested in exploring Mars. Among the hundreds of planets that scientists have discovered orbiting stars outside the solar system, "most are too large, too hot, too cold or not quite right for life as we know it. Mars, though, gets more interesting the closer we look," said research scientist Bethany List Ehlmann.

ChapterThree
RACING TOWARD THE PRIZE

In their pursuit to unlock the mystery of Mars, NASA rovers are on a quest for rocks. They could hold the answer to whether life ever existed on the planet. *Spirit* and *Opportunity* found rocks and minerals strongly suggesting that Mars once held liquid water. *Curiosity*'s primary mission was to find evidence that a watery Mars nourished life.

Scientists debated for five years before deciding that Gale Crater was the best place to look for the story of ancient Mars. There, Mount Sharp's slopes show hundreds of layers, like the colorful bands along Arizona's Grand Canyon. "And you know, geologists, their eyes light up when they see layered rocks, because that's the storybook," explained research scientist Phil Christensen, part of the *Curiosity* team.

Scientists hope Mount Sharp's rocks will explain how Mars became a frigid desert. Geologists believe that over billions of years a lake in the crater could have deposited layers of sand to create sedimentary rock. "Exploring Mount Sharp, we start at the bottom, and we go to the top," said John Grotzinger, the team's chief scientist. "We drive up through the layers, and we turn through the pages and chapters, and we may not finish the book, but I'm sure it's going to be a good read."

Curiosity cast a shadow in the foreground when it photographed its main science target, Mount Sharp.

Powerful orbiter cameras had photographed the layers of Mount Sharp long before *Curiosity* arrived. "The beauty of orbit is you can send a lot of instruments. These orbiters are pretty big," said Christensen. "We've flown cameras that can actually measure the temperature of the surface, lasers that can measure the height of the mountains, and spectrometers that can map what minerals are present. So, from orbit, we can map the entire planet and figure out where all the goodies are." But mission engineer Adam Steltzner explained that "looking from orbit is slightly dissatisfying. It's like window-shopping and never going into the store. So it beckons us down to the surface." Astronauts cannot yet bring back Mars rocks for geologists to study. But rovers can take well-equipped labs to Mars.

A large rover packed with 165 pounds (75 kg) of instruments meant a "big landing problem," Steltzner said. Even landing *Spirit* and *Opportunity*, carrying only 11 pounds (5 kg) of instruments each, had been tricky. Large rocks and unpredictable winds made 80 percent of Mars' surface too dangerous for landing them. "It used to be that we'd show up at Mars and we'd have to roll the dice and hope that Mars wasn't going to kill us," said Steltzner. "We'd just have to hope for good luck."

Airbags had delivered three small rovers safely. But *Curiosity*'s Entry, Descent and Landing team had to invent a new way to land the car-sized rover. "We were kind of backed into this position by the laws of physics," Steltzner said.

EDL team members did not retreat to labs to find a new idea for landing *Curiosity*. Instead Steltzner

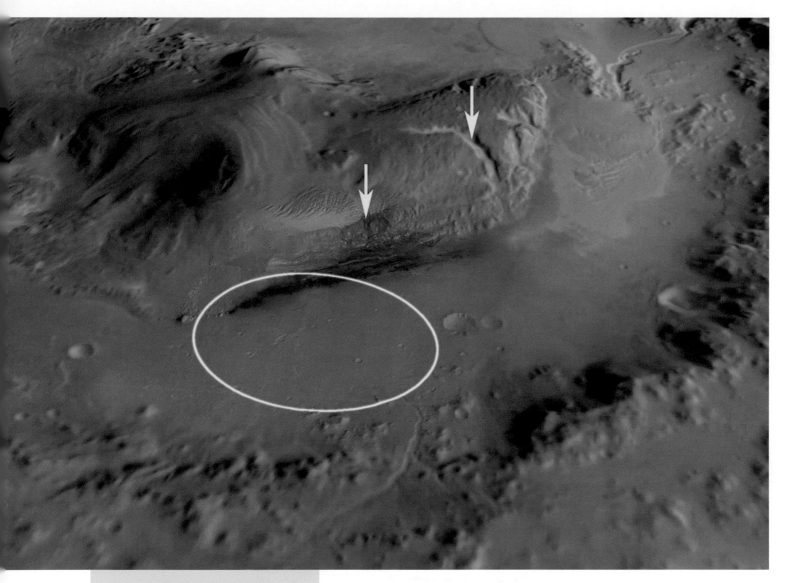

A view of Gale Crater indicates *Curiosity*'s landing site and the mound of layered rocks that scientists study.

described "groups of us throwing ideas around," sharing sketches and computer animations. They also challenged each other. The safety of the rover depended on it. "What I tried to do, as the leader," Steltzner said, "was to offer my own ideas up for attack, to try and engender a culture within the team that was very respectful of individuals, but very aggressive with ideas. We wanted to get rid of the bad

Mission engineer Adam Steltzner demonstrated how *Curiosity* would descend on cables from a sky crane.

ideas. We wanted to be left with the good ideas, and who the good idea came from doesn't really matter."

The team finally settled on a design called the sky crane. It used a sequence of inventive ideas from many engineers. "The way you design something this big is just like your mother taught you how to eat your steak," Steltzner said. "You cut it into small pieces that you can chew. So you break up the task into elements that are attackable by groups of people." Team members worked on various parts of

An artist's concept of a sky crane safely landing *Curiosity* on Mars

the project, from the design of the parachute, rockets, and radar to writing computer code.

From the outset, team members were anxious. "Before it lands successfully, it's unclear whether it's a good idea or a bad idea," Steltzner said. "Was this brilliant or totally stupid?" They had to convince NASA directors that a sky crane was worth testing, a process that would take years and millions of dollars. They cleared that hurdle with a presentation to NASA officials. Steltzner recalled that administrator Mike Griffin said, "I thought it was crazy when they came in here, and after seeing it, I think it still is crazy, but it might be just crazy enough. It might be the right kind of crazy."

But how could the team show that a sky crane was likely to work on Mars? Earth's atmosphere is more than 100 times as dense as that of Mars. "So we have to break the testing down in lots of little pieces, and, by looking at these little individual parts of our testing, convince ourselves the whole will work," said systems engineer Rob Manning. They inflated parachutes in the largest wind tunnel in the world to see whether they would open without tearing. They attached the sky crane's radar to a supersonic jet that plunged from 50,000 feet (15,240 m) to see whether it would measure altitude and speed accurately—as it would need to do while *Curiosity* fell toward Mars' surface. They dropped a rover prototype onto its wheels to see whether the bicycle-inspired titanium frames could absorb the impact.

To test the final part of the landing sequence, scientists headed to California's Mojave Desert. The

A giant parachute dwarfed two engineers as it was being tested for use in a sky crane.

harsh Marslike environment included a crater to simulate where *Curiosity* would land. A helicopter acting as the rocket-powered sky crane lowered a rover prototype on cables to the desert floor.

Applause broke out after successful tests. But

some test results, such as the ripping apart of a parachute in a wind tunnel, left the team disappointed, even heartbroken. "There are moments when you don't know if you have a solution," Steltzner said. "Until you [have] figured out why that went wrong, you don't know if you're going to make it."

Yet disappointments also helped the team make progress. Failures were "usually where we learn our best, most focused lessons," Steltzner said. They also relied on each other. "We took time to be with one another, to enjoy each other's company," he said. "And that bonded us together in those hard times better than any bonding in the good times, and meant that we were resilient to the stress that we would face when we were struggling."

Friendships grew among team members, as did affection for *Curiosity*. Years before fans worldwide became familiar with the robot with humanlike features, mission members began to feel deeply connected to it. "You hear us talk about her as if she's a person, because, to us, she is," said systems engineer Jaime Waydo. Watching *Curiosity* being dropped for landing tests was stressful. "My hands are sweating, and my throat is getting dry," Waydo said. "And then, they let it go, and she hit, and it was so hard. And I was like, 'You can't do that to our baby! That's too much! That's too hard!'"

READING ROCKS

An artist's concept used red to depict the laser beams Curiosity *fires to study minerals.*

Geologists on Earth carry small hammers for breaking rocks open to study their contents. On Mars, *Spirit* and *Opportunity* used wire brushes and grinding tools to remove a rock's dusty, weathered surface. NASA's *Phoenix* Mars lander used a scoop to dig, and it was the first tool to touch frozen water on Mars in 2008. *Curiosity* made history by carrying a drill to Mars.

Curiosity drills precise holes, but scientists are more interested in the pulverized rock left behind. It holds clues about Mars' history. *Curiosity*'s arm delivers powdered rock samples to two labs inside the rover's body. No larger than microwave ovens, they can analyze rocks and air just like chemistry labs on Earth. Instruments shine X-rays at rock samples to determine the structure of their atoms.

A spectrometer shines light at the gas emissions of rock samples heated to 1,800 F (980 C). Individual colors in the light's spectrum either pass through the gas or bounce off. This process determines what minerals are in the rock. One instrument brand-new to Mars can use spectrometry on rocks almost 25 feet (8 m) away. A laser beam shoots from the top of the rover's mast to vaporize and study minerals at a distance. During its first year, the rover fired around 75,000 laser shots.

"I can tell you about the environment that existed 4 billion years ago by looking at what minerals are there," said mission scientist David Blake.

Of course the engineers and scientists thought of *Curiosity* in a practical way too. The rover was a vehicle to carry and protect precious cargo: scientific instruments. Just three months after *Spirit* and *Opportunity* arrived on Mars, NASA held a competition to select proposals for the next rover's instruments. When his instrument was chosen, geochemist Roger Wiens celebrated that his team had won "a ticket to Mars!"

Each team developed and tested its instruments in labs at NASA centers, universities, and private companies across the United States, Canada, and Europe. "The concept of throwing a bunch of engineers together on a project is slightly akin to stranding a group of complete strangers on a desert island," Wiens said. "Things don't necessarily start out smoothly. There are a range of personalities and styles—so many different ways of doing things." But they knew that the 10 instruments aboard *Curiosity* had to work together.

Each instrument team worked to give NASA what its proposals had promised in 2004—a miniature tool that performs a specific task in a harsh environment. They had also promised that the instrument would be affordable to test and build. For years they developed and tested prototypes, adding and removing parts, celebrating when a test worked, shaking their heads when it did not, and trying again. Finally, each team

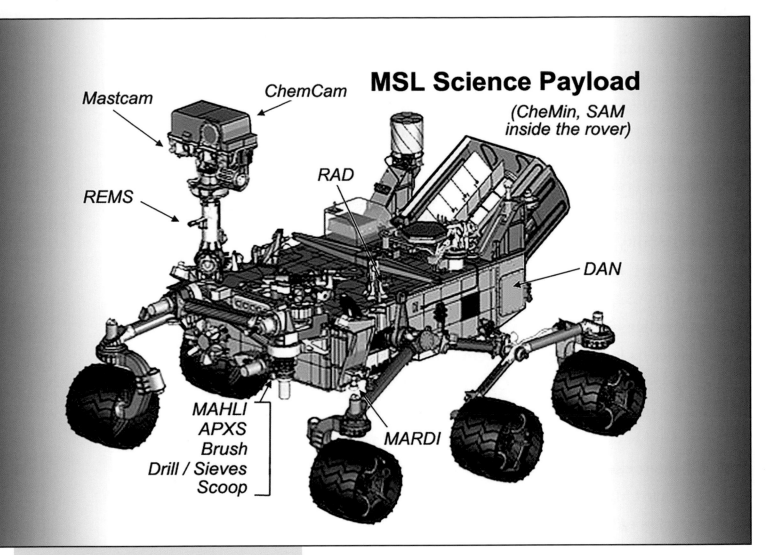

MSL Science Payload

(CheMin, SAM inside the rover)

Mastcam

ChemCam

REMS

RAD

DAN

MAHLI
APXS
Brush
Drill / Sieves
Scoop

MARDI

Curiosity's instruments (clockwise from left): REMS, rover environmental monitoring station; mast camera; chemistry and camera instrument; RAD, radiation assessment detector; CheMin, chemistry and mineralogy instrument; SAM, sample analysis at Mars instrument; DAN, dynamic albedo of neutrons instrument; MARDI, Mars descent imager; MAHLI, Mars hand lens imager; and APXS, alpha particle X-ray spectrometer

sent to JPL a flight model made of durable materials that could withstand space's destructive radiation. The instruments would enable the rover to identify mineral in rock pulverized with a drill or vaporized with a laser. By bouncing neutrons into the ground, *Curiosity* could detect underground water. Its sensors would measure atmospheric pressure, humidity, temperature, wind speeds, and radiation.

At JPL, a team worked on the challenging puzzle of fitting the instruments into *Curiosity*. Wearing white, head-to-toe "clean room suits," they tried to keep microscopic organisms from catching rides to Mars. In dramatic final tests, the rover and its instruments were shaken violently and locked inside a thermal chamber in extreme temperatures to test the rover's ability to survive the difficult journey.

In June 2011, *Curiosity* was transported on an Air Force jet to NASA's Kennedy Space Center in Florida. The last step was installing the nuclear battery that would power its long life on Mars. On November 26, 2011, *Curiosity* waited on Cape Canaveral's launch pad, packed into the top of an Atlas V rocket. As mission members and thousands of spectators watched, the rocket soared up on a plume of fire and shot off toward Mars.

Eight years earlier, engineers had hoped to land *Spirit* and *Opportunity* within target areas of about 50 miles (80 km) long and 7 miles (11 km) wide. With the sky crane, the Mars team believed it could land *Curiosity* inside a much smaller area, just 12 miles (19 km) long by 4 miles (6 km) wide. Their success, Steltzner said, was like "three-pointing a basketball in LA from New York. It's very, very precise."

More than 7,000 scientists and engineers helped design, construct, launch, and land the robot explorer. "We had to come together and let go of our individual

The straight lines in *Curiosity*'s zigzag track marks are Morse code for JPL.

ownership of the pieces, to finally, and collectively, invent something that was none of us, and all of us," Steltzner said. *Curiosity* carries this message wherever it rolls: its wheel treads imprint "JPL" in Morse code in the Martian sand.

ChapterFour
THE HUNT FOR SIGNS OF LIFE

Curiosity made headlines with its heart-thumping plunge to Mars. For years since then, it has rolled quietly around Mars at an average speed of just half an inch (1 cm) per second. Yet the rover still thrills audiences. Systems engineer Allen Chen said "it's like Christmas every day" as the rover's data and new images—more than 72,000 just in its first year—arrive on Earth.

Curiosity sends back data from which scientists create complex graphs of the measurements taken by its instruments. But it also sends beautiful photographs of wind-shaped dunes and colorful rocks. "When you see those foothills," said chief scientist John Grotzinger, "it looks like a familiar place. It's like you'd almost come home, in a way, to a different part of the Earth, except this is Mars." The red planet is much smaller than Earth, but both have about the same size land surface. They both have four seasons, since their rotational axes have similar tilts. Polar ice caps cover their tops and bottoms. But on Mars the polar ice caps contain carbon dioxide ice as well as water ice.

The rover's photographs also show a haunting portrait of Mars. The only evidence of movement is wind across a dry landscape. *Curiosity*'s sensors

A composite image of photos taken from NASA orbiters allows viewers an understanding of the relative sizes of Earth and Mars. Oceans cover much of Earth's surface.

also take precise measurements of the effects of its meager atmosphere. Temperatures can dive to -284 F (-175 C). Radiation levels are dangerously high for any living organism. In contrast, Earth's dense atmosphere nurtures countless life forms. Water shapes the landscape constantly through rain, waves, and floods.

Curiosity's mast camera took photos of sedimentary deposits in Gale Crater.

Yet scientists increasingly believe that at one time, the planets were not very different. "To some extent, Mars is like a twin of Earth, early in its history," Grotzinger said. This theory drives scientists to pay close attention to Mars. "By going to Gale Crater and looking at sediments and rocks that are very old, we're getting not only a snapshot of early Mars, but also a snapshot of what early Earth might have looked like at the time when we think life evolved," said mission scientist David Blake.

The Mars Reconnaissance Orbiter was launched in 2005. As it orbits Mars, it searches for evidence that water persisted on the planet for long periods of time.

Since *Mariner 4*, scientists have studied one of Earth's closest neighbors so carefully that in "many ways Mars is better mapped than Earth, as no features are hidden from study," said planetary cartographer Matt Chwastyk. Yet the planet still hides a great mystery. On Earth, life appeared about 3.8 billion years ago as microscopic microbes. What about on Mars? Even if the simplest life forms developed on Mars, said astrophysicist Melissa Rice, "doesn't that make it more likely that primitive life could be emerging on planets around stars throughout the universe? And if primitive life is more likely throughout the universe, doesn't it make it more possible that at least one planet has evolved life similar to us? Intelligent life that maybe, someday, we could talk to? This is why Mars is so important."

Curiosity's instruments search for small pieces to the greatest puzzle of all: Are we alone? "I think it's the grandest of all scientific questions," Grotzinger said. Yet scientists are not hopeful about finding traces of living or ancient Martian microbes, at least not near the surface. When Mars' atmosphere thinned out, the planet lost its protection against radiation traveling through space. These particles, which are smaller than atoms, can break down any biological matter. Radiation can travel through human skin and destroy cells, for example. On Mars, radiation could have destroyed microbes and even ancient microfossils.

Instead of looking for microbes, *Curiosity* scientists set out to search for the ingredients needed for life. On Earth, the recipe calls for liquid water and a source of energy for microbial life. *Curiosity* found the marks of liquid water in many places in Gale Crater. Its photographs show rocks piling up like pieces of broken concrete. Rounded edges tell scientists that the rocks once tumbled through water. "Most people are familiar with rounded river pebbles.

Are we alone? "I think it's the grandest of all scientific questions."

ROVING MARS

Bright powder in the foreground indicates where Curiosity *reached down to drill into Martian rock.*

Each morning *Curiosity* receives instructions from Earth through its antennae. The message, in computer code, is the result of careful planning on Earth. Rover teams use many ways to guess at what *Curiosity* will find in its path. They need to steer it clear of jagged rocks, up the steep slopes of Mount Sharp, and toward interesting rocks for sampling. They study the rover's most recent photographs and practice navigating through computer simulations. At the Jet Propulsion Laboratory's simulated Martian landscape, the Mars Yard, rover team members practice navigating a rover model over rocks and sand.

Because of the time delay between the planets, rover drivers once preprogrammed the rover's activities for the entire day, just as engineers preprogrammed its descent. But in 2013 *Curiosity*'s computer software was upgraded to allow "autonomous navigation," which means it can drive itself at times. Now rover team members can give *Curiosity* a destination and let the rover choose the best path.

Using two cameras mounted on its mast, *Curiosity* can map the terrain ahead in three dimensions. If the rover can make driving decisions in real time, it might be able to avoid dangers like the soft sand that trapped *Spirit*'s wheel.

Curiosity found evidence of an ancient flowing stream on Mars. The size and rounded shape of gravel are key indicators.

Maybe you've picked up a smoothed, round rock to skip across the water. Seeing something so familiar on another world is exciting and also gratifying,"

Scientists say Mars probably once swirled with ocean water.

said scientist Rebecca Williams of the Planetary Science Institute. She calculated that at one time, a stream in Gale Crater "was flowing at a speed equivalent to a walking pace—a meter, or three feet, per second—and it was ankle-deep to hip-deep."

Scientists wondered whether this water had been too salty or acidic to host life. After *Curiosity*'s cameras photographed fine-grained sedimentary rocks formed by flowing water, the rover drilled. X-rays and spectrometry of the powdered sample revealed one of Gale Crater's secrets. It contained clay and minerals formed in water that might have been low enough in acid and salt to be habitable. After all, some microbes on Earth can survive in harsh conditions such as in the acidic, scalding water of hot springs.

Based on *Curiosity*'s data, mission scientists made an announcement in October 2015. About 3.5 billion years ago, they said, rivers and lakes in Gale Crater dropped sand and pebbles that gradually built the lower layers of Mount Sharp. Scientists say Mars probably once swirled with ocean water. Data from *Curiosity*, *Opportunity*, and orbiters tell scientists that an ocean most likely covered half of Mars' northern area, and that it was more than a mile deep.

How do scientists know about this ancient ocean? Martian rocks help answer that question. *Curiosity* can compare the composition of the planet's air today with the air of ancient Mars. Its lab instruments heat up rock samples to release gases that have been trapped inside for billions of years. Spectrometers measure the amounts of elements such as hydrogen, carbon, and oxygen. When they compare Mars' air today with ancient air, scientists can tell that Mars once had a dense atmosphere. It allowed oceans, lakes, and rivers to form.

Life-forms on Earth depend on more than water. They need certain chemicals as building blocks and also for food. *Curiosity*'s scientists searched for the chemicals that make life possible on Earth and found them in a sample drilled from Mars' clay-rich rock. Using data from the rover's lab, scientists identified nitrogen, sulfur, hydrogen, oxygen, phosphorus, and carbon. "A fundamental question for this mission is whether Mars could have supported a habitable environment," said NASA scientist Michael Meyer. "From what we know now, the answer is yes."

Yet scientists are far from finished with the *Curiosity* mission. "We think life began on Earth around 3.8 billion years ago, and our result shows that places on Mars had the same conditions at that time—liquid water, a warm environment, and organic matter," said NASA scientist Caroline Freissinet. "So if life emerged on Earth in these conditions, why not on Mars as well?" Mars teases scientists with mysterious clues. *Curiosity* found complex molecules

"A fundamental question for this mission is whether Mars could have supported a habitable environment. From what we know now, the answer is yes."

The Mars hand lens imager captured *Curiosity* at a drilling site.

composed of carbon, hydrogen, and oxygen in a rock sample. These organic molecules are some of the building blocks for Earth's life-forms. But scientists are cautious because some chemical reactions can produce organic molecules in water without the presence of life.

Scientists also puzzle over measurements of methane gas that rise and fall in Mars' air. On Earth, living organisms produce this gas when they digest food. Could microbes be living under the Martian surface? Maybe, but scientists know that other chemical reactions can also produce methane. "It's as if Mars is challenging us, saying, 'Hey, find out what this means,'" said scientist Michael Mumma.

To continue the search for microbial life, scientists will need another rover. "Even though the *Curiosity* rover has the most sophisticated instruments ever sent to Mars, they're already out of date," said astrophysicist Melissa Rice in 2015. NASA plans to launch a rover similar to *Curiosity* in 2020. It will also help store samples from Mars for a future mission that is expected to return them to Earth. "We need [Mars'] rocks here to keep pace with the newest technology," said Rice.

NASA's scientists and engineers hope their robots will pave the way for people to land on Mars in the 2030s. The next rover will test technology to produce oxygen and locate water to help future explorers live on the inhospitable planet. But for now, *Curiosity*'s images continue to take scientists and viewers on a trip to Mars. Systems geologist Ken Edgett finds

Earth

Curiosity's mast camera photo of the Martian horizon and sky includes Earth as the brightest point in the night sky.

inspiration in a special portrait taken by the rover. In a photo taken after sunset from Gale Crater, Earth and its moon appear as bright "evening stars" in the Martian night sky. "This is why we do this," said Edgett. "It's really for understanding our home."

Timeline

1957

The Soviet Union launches *Sputnik I*, the first artificial satellite to orbit Earth; *Sputnik II*, launched later in the year, carries the first space traveler, a dog named Laika

1958

The United States launches its first satellite, *Explorer 1*; the National Aeronautics and Space Administration (NASA) is formed

1969

U.S. astronauts Neil Armstrong and Edwin "Buzz" Aldrin are the first people to land on the moon

1971

The American probe *Mariner 9* orbits Mars and transmits thousands of images of the red planet; the Soviet probe *Mars 3* lands on Mars and sends a brief transmission to Earth before losing contact

1961

Soviet cosmonaut Yuri Gagarin is the first human to enter space; in 1963 Soviet cosmonaut Valentina Tereshkova becomes the first woman in space

1965

The American space probe *Mariner 4* takes the first detailed photos of Mars

1976

NASA puts two landers on Mars, *Viking 1* and *Viking 2*; they take detailed color photographs of Mars' landscape and search for evidence of microbial life

1997

Mars *Pathfinder* and its rover *Sojourner* arrive on Mars and find evidence that water once flowed on the planet

Timeline

2001

Mars *Odyssey* orbiter maps minerals on the planet's surface from space; *Odyssey* later played an important communications role during the Mars Science Laboratory mission to land *Curiosity*

2004

The rovers *Spirit* and *Opportunity* continue the search for evidence of water on Mars

2013

Curiosity confirms that Gale Crater could have hosted microbial life on ancient Mars

2014

The *MAVEN* (Mars Atmosphere and Volatile Evolution Mission) orbiter enters Mars orbit to search for clues about Mars' dramatic climate change

2008

The *Phoenix* lander arrives in Mars' north polar region to study ice-filled soil

2012

NASA's Mars Science Laboratory lands the *Curiosity* rover to search for clues that Mars could have supported microscopic life forms

2016

NASA approves a 2018 launch of its *InSight* lander mission to study the deep interior of Mars

2017

Work continues on NASA's plan to launch a $2 billion rover in 2020 to search for signs of life on Mars and to collect and store samples for their future return to Earth

Glossary

biological—having to do with life

dust devil—small whirlwind over land, visible as a column of dust and debris

electromagnetic radiation—form of energy that includes visible light, infrared light, ultraviolet light, radio waves, microwaves, X-rays, and gamma rays

elements—basic chemical substances that cannot be broken down into simpler substances

microbe—very tiny living thing

microfossil—microscopic remains of an ancient plant or animal that has hardened into rock

molecule—smallest particle into which a substance can be divided without being changed chemically

neutron—particle in the nucleus of an atom that has no electric charge

orbiter—spacecraft that travels around a planet or other space object

organic molecules—molecules that contain the element carbon, which is found in all living things

panoramic—wide, sweeping

probe—spacecraft sent to gather data

prototype—first trial model of something, made to test and improve the design

spectrometer—instrument that measures the intensity of light at various wavelengths

Additional Resources

Further Reading

Aldrin, Buzz, and Marianne J. Dyson. *Welcome to Mars: Making a Home on the Red Planet.* Washington, D.C.: National Geographic, 2015.

Miller, Ron. Curiosity's *Mission on Mars: Exploring the Red Planet.* Minneapolis: Twenty-First Century Books, 2014.

Rusch, Elizabeth. *The Mighty Mars Rovers: The Incredible Adventures of* Spirit *and* Opportunity. Boston: Houghton Mifflin Books for Children, 2012.

Internet Sites

Use FactHound to find Internet sites related to this book.
Visit *www.facthound.com*
Just type in 9780756556419 and go.

Critical Thinking Questions

In what ways do you think exploring Mars has improved life on Earth, or could improve it? Consider the effects on scientists, people in general, and the environment.

How has failure helped Mars exploration to progress? Consider the history of Mars exploration and the recent experiences of scientists and engineers working on *Curiosity*'s mission. Use examples from the text to support your answer.

The names of Mars rovers and landers seem unscientific. Explain why you think these names were selected. Consider the attitudes toward Mars exploration of both the mission teams and the public.

Source Notes

Page 4, line 21: Roger Wiens. *Red Rover: Inside the Story of Robotic Space Exploration, from Genesis to the Mars Rover Curiosity*. New York: Basic Books, 2013, p. 160.

Page 6, line 1: Jennifer Chu. "MIT alums recount their Martian experiences." Massachusetts Institute of Technology News Office. 11 Oct. 2012. 13 Jan. 2017. http://news.mit.edu/2012/curious-aeroastro-alum-event-1011

Page 6, line 8: Jacqueline Howard. "Mars Rover Curiosity Video: NASA Scientists Call Landing Sequence 'Seven Minutes Of Terror.'" *The Huffington Post*. 26 June 2012. 13 Jan. 2017. http://www.huffingtonpost.com/2012/06/25/mars-curiosity-rover-video-nasa-landing-terror_n_1626067.html

Page 6, line 19: Ultimate Mars Challenge. *Nova*. PBS. 14 Nov. 2012. 13 Jan. 2017. http://www.pbs.org/wgbh/nova/space/ultimate-mars-challenge.html

Page 7, line 3: "Where Were You When *Curiosity* Landed on Mars?" Transcript. Jet Propulsion Lab. California Institute of Technology. 15 Aug. 2012. 16 Jan. 2017. http://www.jpl.nasa.gov/video/details.php?id=1116

Page 7, line 7: "Challenges of Getting to Mars: *Curiosity*'s Seven Minutes of Terror." NASA. 22 June 2012. 16 Jan. 2017. https://www.youtube.com/watch?v=OHwUrxzrvtg

Page 9, col. 1, line 9: *Red Rover: Inside the Story of Robotic Space Exploration, from Genesis to the Mars Rover Curiosity*, p. 168.

Page 9, col. 2, line 6: "Adam Steltzner on the search for life on Mars." The New Yorker Festival. 22 July 2014. 16 Jan. 2017. https://www.youtube.com/watch?v=oYrygqiZeCo

Page 10, line 1: "Challenges of Getting to Mars: *Curiosity*'s Seven Minutes of Terror."

Page 10, line 3: "Where Were You When *Curiosity* Landed on Mars?"

Page 10, line 18: "Adam Steltzner on the search for life on Mars."

Page 10, line 23: "Where Were You When *Curiosity* Landed on Mars?"

Page 10, line 28: R. Aileen Yingst. "A View of the *Curiosity* Rover from MAHLI." TedX Talks. 8 Dec. 2014. 16 Jan. 2017. https://www.youtube.com/watch?v=AiRavXSFY0I

Page 11, line 4: *Red Rover: Inside the Story of Robotic Space Exploration, from Genesis to the Mars Rover Curiosity*, p. 208.

Page 12, line 1: Adam Steltzner. "How the Trip to Mars has Changed Us." Tedx Talks. 15 Jan. 2013. 16 Jan. 2017. https://www.youtube.com/watch?v=l9P9JNwwiMY

Page 12, line 19: Emi Kolawole. "Mars rover *Curiosity* approaches the Red Planet (live blog). *The Washington Post*. 6 Aug. 2012. 16 Jan. 2017. https://www.washingtonpost.com/blogs/innovations/post/mars-rover-curiosity-approaches-the-red-planet-live/2012/08/05/c51c9068-dd8c-11e1-af1d-753c613ff6d8_blog.html?utm_term=.ad5ebb2f6af6

Page 12, line 23: "A View of the *Curiosity* Rover from MAHLI."

Page 29, line 7: Fraser Cain. "*Opportunity* is Parked at the Shore of an Ancient Martian Sea." Universe Today. 19 Dec. 2015. 19 Jan. 2017. http://www.universetoday.com/9427/opportunity-is-parked-at-the-shore-of-an-ancient-martian-sea/

Page 29, line 10: Mars Rovers: *Opportunity*. Exploring the Planets. Smithsonian National Air and Space Museum. 19 Jan. 2017. https://airandspace.si.edu/exhibitions/exploring-the-planets/online/solar-system/mars/observations/opportunity.cfm

Page 29, line 14: Ibid.

Page 29, line 23: Bethany List Ehlmann. "My Year on Mars as a member of the *Curiosity* rover team." *The Guardian*. 5 Aug. 2013. 19 Jan. 2017. https://www.theguardian.com/commentisfree/2013/aug/05/mars-curiosity-rover-anniversary-accompliments

Page 30, line 12: Ultimate Mars Challenge.

Page 30, line 20: Ibid.

Page 31, line 3: Ibid.

Page 32, line 7: Adam Steltzner. "How *Curiosity* Changed My Life, and I Changed Hers." TEDx Talks. 19 Nov. 2012. 25 Jan. 2017. https://www.youtube.com/watch?v=IvhurxOxid0

Page 32, line 13: "Adam Steltzner on the search for life on Mars."

Page 32, line 18: Ibid.

Page 32, line 25: Ibid.

Page 33, line 1: Ibid.

Page 33, line 4: "How the Trip to Mars has Changed Us."

Page 34, line 5: "Adam Steltzner on the search for life on Mars."

Page 35, line 4: Ibid.

Page 36, line 7: Ibid.

Page 36, line 13: Ultimate Mars Challenge.

Page 38, line 3: "Adam Steltzner on the search for life on Mars."

Page 38, line 8: Ibid.

Page 38, line 10: "How the Trip to Mars has Changed Us."

Page 38, line 19: Ultimate Mars Challenge.

Page 38, line 22: Ibid.

Page 39, col. 2, line 11: Nola Taylor Redd. "Curious About Life: Interview with David Blake." *Astrobiology Magazine*. 20 Sept. 2012. 25 Jan. 2017. http://www.astrobio.net/interview/curious-about-life-interview-with-david-blake/

Page 40, line 9: *Red Rover: Inside the Story of Robotic Space Exploration, from Genesis to the Mars Rover Curiosity*, p. 109.

Page 40, line 13: Ibid., p. 112.

Page 42, line 24: "Adam Steltzner on the search for life on Mars."

Page 42, line 28: "How the Trip to Mars has Changed Us."

Page 44, line 5: "MIT alums recount their Martian experiences."

Page 44, line 13: Ultimate Mars Challenge.

Page 46, line 2: Ibid.

Page 46, line 5: "Curious About Life: Interview with David Blake."

Page 47, line 3: Betsy Mason. "What Mars Maps Got Right (and Wrong) Through Time." *National Geographic*. 19 Oct. 2016. 25 Jan. 2017. http://news.nationalgeographic.com/2016/10/planets-maps-exploring-mars-space-science/

Page 47, line 10: Melissa Rice. "Bringing Mars to Earth: NASA's next Rover Mission." TEDx Talks. 23 June 2015. 23 Jan. 2017. https://www.youtube.com/watch?v=hunfKE7ZE28

Page 48, line 9: Ultimate Mars Challenge.

Page 48, line 28: "Pebbly Rocks Testify to Old Streambed on Mars." Mars Science Lab. Jet Propulsion Lab. California Institute of Technology. 30 May 2013. 25 Jan. 2017. http://mars.nasa.gov/msl/news/whatsnew/index.cfm?FuseAction=ShowNews&NewsID=1477

Page 51, line 3: Ibid.

Page 52, line 16: "NASA Rover Finds Conditions Once Suited for Ancient Life on Mars." Mars Science Lab. Jet Propulsion Lab. California Institute of Technology. 12 March 2013. 24 Jan. 2017. http://mars.nasa.gov/msl/news/whatsnew/index.cfm?FuseAction=ShowNews&NewsID=1438

Page 52, line 21: "How NASA *Curiosity* Instrument Made First Detection of Organic Matter on Mars." Jet Propulsion Laboratory, California Institute of Technology. 16 Dec. 2014. 24 Jan. 2017. http://www.jpl.nasa.gov/news/news.php?feature=4414

Page 54, line 9: "Martian Methane Reveals the Red Planet is not a Dead Planet." Mars: NASA Explores the Red Planet. 15 Jan. 2009. 24 Jan. 2017. http://www.nasa.gov/mission_pages/mars/news/marsmethane.html

Page 54, line 13: "Bringing Mars to Earth: NASA's next Rover Mission."

Page 54, line 19: Ibid.

Page 55, line 4 "Mars Up Close, Part 3: Ken Edgett." National Geographic Live. 3 Nov. 2014. 6 March 2017. https://www.youtube.com/watch?v=-Ajfql6CirE 9:03

Select Bibliography

"Adam Steltzner on the search for life on Mars." The New Yorker Festival. 22 July 2014. 16 Jan. 2017. https://www.youtube.com/watch?v=oYrygqiZeCo

Cain, Fraser. "Opportunity is Parked at the Shore of an Ancient Martian Sea." Universe Today. 19 Dec. 2015. 19 Jan. 2017. http://www.universetoday.com/9427/opportunity-is-parked-at-the-shore-of-an-ancient-martian-sea/

"Challenges of Getting to Mars: *Curiosity*'s Seven Minutes of Terror." NASA. 22 June 2012. 16 Jan. 2017. https://www.youtube.com/watch?v=OHwUrxzrvtg

A Chronology of Mars Exploration. NASA History Program Office. 25 April 2017. http://history.nasa.gov/marschro.htm

Chu, Jennifer. "MIT alums recount their Martian experiences." Massachusetts Institute of Technology News Office. 11 Oct. 2012. 13 Jan. 2017. http://news.mit.edu/2012/curious-aeroastro-alum-event-1011

Ehlmann, Bethany List. "My Year on Mars as a member of the *Curiosity* rover team." *The Guardian*. 5 Aug. 2013. 19 Jan. 2017. https://www.theguardian.com/commentisfree/2013/aug/05/mars-curiousity-rover-anniversary-accoumplisments

Exploring the Planets. Mars. Smithsonian National Air and Space Museum. 25 April 2017. https://airandspace.si.edu/exhibitions/exploring-the-planets/online/solar-system/mars/

Howard, Jacqueline. "Mars Rover *Curiosity* Video: NASA Scientists Call Landing Sequence 'Seven Minutes of Terror.'" *The Huffington Post*. 26 June 2012. 13 Jan. 2017. http://www.huffingtonpost.com/2012/06/25/mars-curiosity-rover-video-nasa-landing-terror_n_1626067.html

Journey to Mars. NASA. 25 April 2017. https://www.nasa.gov/topics/journeytomars/index.html

Kolawole, Emi. "Mars rover *Curiosity* approaches the Red Planet (live blog). *The Washington Post*. 6 Aug. 2012. 16 Jan. 2017. https://www.washingtonpost.com/blogs/innovations/post/mars-rover-curiosity-approaches-the-red-planet-live/2012/08/05/c51c9068-dd8c-11e1-af1d-753c613ff6d8_blog.html?utm_term=.ad5ebb2f6af6

Madrigal, Alexis C. "From *Sojourner* to *Curiosity*: A Mars Rover Family Portrait." *The Atlantic*. 6 Aug. 2012. 25 April 2017. http://www.theatlantic.com/technology/archive/2012/08/from-sojourner-to-curiosity-a-mars-rover-family-portrait/260779/

Mars Exploration. NASA. 25 April 2017. https://mars.nasa.gov

Mason, Betsy. "What Mars Maps Got Right (and Wrong) Through Time." *National Geographic*. 19 Oct. 2016. 25 Jan. 2017. http://news.nationalgeographic.com/2016/10/planets-maps-exploring-mars-space-science/

Redd, Nola Taylor. "Curious About Life: Interview with David Blake." *Astrobiology Magazine*. 20 Sept. 2012. 25 Jan. 2017. http://www.astrobio.net/interview/curious-about-life-interview-with-david-blake/

Steltzner, Adam. "How *Curiosity* Changed My Life, and I Changed Hers." TEDx Talks. 19 Nov. 2012. 25 Jan. 2017. https://www.youtube.com/watch?v=IvhurxOxid0

Steltzner, Adam, and William Patrick. *The Right Kind of Crazy: A True Story of Teamwork, Leadership, and High-Stakes Innovation*. New York: Portfolio/Penguin, 2016.

Ultimate Mars Challenge. *Nova*. PBS. 14 Nov. 2012. 13 Jan. 2017. http://www.pbs.org/wgbh/nova/space/ultimate-mars-challenge.html

"Where Were You When Curiosity Landed on Mars?" Transcript. Jet Propulsion Lab. California Institute of Technology. 15 Aug. 2012. 16 Jan. 2017. http://www.jpl.nasa.gov/video/details.php?id=1116

Wiens, Roger. Red Rover: *Inside the Story of Robotic Space Exploration, from* Genesis *to the Mars Rover* Curiosity. New York: Basic Books, 2013.

Yingst, R. Aileen. "A View of the *Curiosity* Rover from MAHLI." TedX Talks. 8 Dec. 2014. 16 Jan. 2017. https://www.youtube.com/watch?v=AiRavXSFY0I

Index

About the Author

As a former teacher, Danielle Smith-Llera taught children to think and write about literature before writing books for them herself. As the spouse of a diplomat, she enjoys living in both Washington, D.C., and overseas in countries such as India, Jamaica, and Romania.